# BRAN̶    ̶D
# THAT PLACE
# OF LITTLE GREEN POEMS

# G W COLKITTO

Cinnamon Press
:: small miracles from distinctive voices ::

Published by Cinnamon Press
Meirion House,
Glan yr afon,
Tanygrisiau
Blaenau Ffestiniog,
Gwynedd, LL41 3SU
www.cinnamonpress.com

The right of G.W. Colkitto to be identified as author of this work has been asserted by him in accordance with the Copyright, Designs and Patent Act, 1988. Copyright © 2019 G. W. Colkitto
ISBN: 978-1-78864-065-7

British Library Cataloguing in Publication Data. A CIP record for this book can be obtained from the British Library.

Designed and typeset in Palatino by Cinnamon Press.
Cover design by Adam Craig from artwork by G W Colkitto

Printed in Poland

Cinnamon Press is represented in the UK by Inpress Ltd and in Wales by the Welsh Books Council.

## Acknowledgements

'At Coniston' and 'At Night on Return Home from Brantwood' were first published in *Waitin tae meet wie the Dei*l (diehard)

## Brantwood: That Place Of Little Green Poems

Little Green Poems arrived from the unknown; words prompted by Pippa Little and Geraldine Green to the backdrop of Coniston Water and Ruskin's home at Brantwood.

These poems unfolded with the encouragement of Geraldine and Pippa and the friendship of the other poets on the same journey. All, were written over six days of poetry, three in 2017 and three in 2018.

I see them arranged in a vase on a mosaic table at the window of the Studio Kitchen, Brantwood. These are the grasses from the wild-flower meadow, the corn strung clouds reflected in the Lake. The neon damsel fly gone before it can be caught in a photograph.

Please come with me to that strange landscape where physical blends with mystical.

*G.W. Colkitto*

# Contents

## June 2017

## June 2018

Brantwood:
that place of
little green poems

*To Allan and Robert,*
*who are always there for me.*

June 2017

# Brantwood

I did not see the glacier bound rocks
I did not see the melting land rebound
nor did I see the first green creeping plant
nor did I see man laying out his walls
but I did see the folded grey water
but I did see the quarry on the hill
but I did see high chimneys against the blast
but I did see the village shadowed down
but I did see the painted harlot lake
and I remembered how I loved and why
and I remembered why trees reach up to the sky

# At Coniston

the Old Man has cooried doon under
a muslin sheet
I cannot see his clouded brow
but know he has not moved
waits passing rain
will stare back at me
haunting Ruskin's home
rubbing dry thoughts into sparks of verse
trying to light my fire
he has seen reputations crash and burn
counted walkers out and back
comforted city casualties
who come to nature's ward of solitude
he gathers them to the fold
till they are hefted on his shoulders
I sit in the Professor's bower
held tight in stone
taste smoke upon my lips
blow word rings on the page
wait for the paper to scorch
but this day's mist dampens my chance of flame
I retreat to the House
to a circle of friends
to hunker down in their warmth

# It is written in the arch of the sky—John Ruskin

their name escapes me in the sun
my shadowed memory losing where I stored
this shape of fading lilac
sun-bleached     month withered
they hang their skirts in dry surrender

beyond the pergola     fuchsia bee-tremble
nod to waving birch and ash
the lake plays hide and seek
behind a lime screen

I count colours in the Professor's Garden
six tones of purple     three shades of pink
two yellows and so many greens
I abandon need

through my shadows Clematis cling to the pergola
leaves breeze pattern the page of the sky
dapple the path

I smile at remembering
that recaptured name
smile for that smile

smile for tomorrow
when I will sit in other shadows
remember this

# No Dragon Slain

I take her chained heart
pin it to my Peacock waistcoat
buttons strain as I proudly strut
the gold ring embedded in the flesh torn flesh
shivers as it beats on in feeble misery
her outstretched hand is stained with tears
but I brush her aside
to watch my confidence

her body belongs where I lay it
and I carry her heart as an emblem
that blood which seeps into the cloth
unimportant

I can boast of how I slayed the maid
my foot upon her neck will not be moved
by any need for valour
for she will never find the fire
to rise again

## Laced tight

boots take me where
I follow the signs and the prepared
surface of slate grey grit
a marker says 2/3 of a mile
and I recalculate my steps from
when I would cover in twelve minutes
to a cortège half hour

the evening is comfortable
my stride set by heart and lung
my eyes on the next gate
although I let the fields and sky
the chewing cow intrude
for their smile

the boots plod on
at this funereal pace
until my resting place
where I find my elixir
The Church Inn sells real ale
my path home lighter
boots lifted higher
by pints of heavy

# I paint it black

the front door remembers
what I try to forget
every creak as it is pushed
tells of age and how age comes

hinges resist but yield to pressure
shoulder to the Oak   dead Oak
yet somehow still alive
in tight grained strength

polished smooth from countless hands
who entered here in hope
who angry flung it crashing
but did not split its certainty

holding out the out
hiding in the in
remembers all the come and go
frames time and place

# Rocking Horse

this day is his father
sires breaks and shocks
stones clatter hoof beats
stones breaking his line
which falls and rises
rolls on into time
when he was sane
when his Dad held the reins
now he slides into madness
nothing stays where he sits
he swings to and fro
never has peace

# Dreams unowned

*All breakages will be paid*

*after lines by Charles Wright—*
> *'You caught it here in the…'*
> *and: 'all of this which lies behind me'*

you caught it here
in slip clay on the pot
in white gloss on brick rust

simple
it seems simple
and yet I can hold you
finger your fingers in the clay
feel it turn in your hand
watch you lift from the kiln
perfect   no cracks on body
glazed as you hoped

now in my hands
here in the boot sale
I can for a token
buy your imagination

and I then see you
hunched over the wheel
throwing raw clay
dead centre
it lives and you are dead
I put it back on the stall
unable to trust I will not break it
hurry to look at electric nothings
leave these dreams unowned

all this lies behind me
as I close the car door
drive home to the bare shelf
where you could have had honoured place
if I had not feared your haunting
the way you had slipped under my breath
embraced me in iron-stone

# Thoughts at the Studio Window

four igneous slabs
a dislodged roof
memory of bones


burrow in a barrow
thoughts wheel into distance
time unwrapped


drawn to the opposite
seeking magnetic south
am I alone searching
for a route to the underworld


they could not find me
gave up    went home
I won this time    gloated
until I found isolation
no comfort

# At Night on Return Home from Brantwood

my madness plays black-gammon with Ruskin's daemon
which surprises me as I do not know the rules
only know this daemon from the abandoned bedroom

high
        floating high
                a window floating

realise there is no rule of black

step back
to watch wraith touch wraith
in consolation of dream and dark caverns
unruled passages of night

my madness sees mourn irises caressed by Ruskin's eye
hears a sigh leave the perfect window

  picture
        in my vision
              of this dream

ghost down the path to the constant lake

we walk on water
like a god with stylus in hand
chip chip at alabaster

seeking   seeking

madness turns to me says go to sleep

I want to leave the flowers delicate
arranged on mosaic table
in the window close pained

                                    [...]

drift and drift
        find
                no
    do not find

       a final line

June 2018

# Winter in the Circus of Melancholia

December is no time to learn the unicycle
an accident in waiting a pain in the proverbial
fool to disregard warnings
days of fluked success lead to falling

walk the tightrope spin the top
there is nothing childish in failure
nothing grown-up with trick cyclists
drunk and sober the sombre truth
clowns hide their pain in foolishness

when you enter the Big Top peddling
suspended over that shimmering shaft
the assembled throng are willing you to stumble
your frantic feet spinning ever faster
while in that game of chance your empty bottle
comes to rest on cheap laughs

you force a chuckle from the pain
take a stiff bow
there are more rings to enter
more trapeze to swing from
retouch the mask
you cannot leave the spotlight
until the elephants dance a tango

## Thoughts from Gillian Allnut:
### I have a new river now

storm gouged
cut a different channel
the land does not lie

in the eddy
twisting under bare roots
a swirl of leaves

bank on this
flood tears the barriers
bricks do not float

# Howling Dog

you shout my name in the night
curse my bones  the moon split clouds
curse my birth ask for my death

shut in behind brick and glass you hate
my ancient prayers my wild understanding
of shadows of scents you only dream

you know your blindness
how fear creeps behind eyelids
crawls under rib nibbles your nakedness
when I all fur and tooth
throw back my head and howl
it tells you beware what is unseen
tells you I am not afraid
to face what you cannot
and rage at your impotence

# Diving Shipwrecks

*From George Wallace:*
>*You and Me Dad — we have done our time diving shipwrecks*

What age was I, eight nine?
Does it matter? It was you, me and Allan, Robert,
going to see where you worked.
I never asked, but guess they had been before,
but not I, until that day, sixty years ago, or more.
Depends when this is read. Or should it be when I write it?
Does it matter? It is a memory every son wants
of his father, of the place where he earned the money,
that paid for ice creams, the big wooden yo-yo, for the bike
and the weekly comics, for the holidays on Arran.
I knew all this, for Mum told me, told me of the hours,
the study, told me of your right hand so much larger than your left
from hard labour from when you were fourteen.
Does it matter? That I remember the men boiler-suited grim
but laughing. The noise, so I could not hear the swearing,
though, in those distant days, I doubt they swore when I was there.
You didn't swear when women or children were in earshot.
Does it matter? That I remember the Board Room, all dark wood
walls, polished table and special chair with arms and higher back
for the owner, the man who owned your job, your time.
Does it matter, Dad? That I see you young, see me small
and know this never changed. No matter the shipyard went.
The job went. You went. Mum went. All slipped under the years,
the seas that drown us all. Does it matter? That I rarely swim down
into those reefs of childhood. You made a boat for me, handed me the oars,
said, the horizon is yours, and I rowed over the lip of the world
into…

# To the Dog Tag

when they open the box of rings
engagement   wedding   showy black-banded
they will find you
cheap yellow plastic   with broken circle
of failed metal

they will recognise my faded fading
illegible scrawl trying neatness
trapped behind clear cover     the name
the last of six dogs (if they can work that out)
remember an old terrier reluctant to let go

they will not see the sprightly pup
the fast striding walk     nor remember
me running with you on a never-ending beach
they will not see you climb on Margaret's knee
or hear her laugh as you kiss her face

the address they will recall (from years ago)
not where you made your bed     nor where you fed
they may draw up other names share a few words
before tossing aside as worthless scrap

I (on the other hand) with rings and stones
value you like diamond.

# The Hut

in this summer brightness
I am a pup again with Dad
outside the garden shed as he saws
to fix a step for me to mount
the rocking horse whose head he crafted
in the shed at his vice
whose eye he painted and whose reins
made of ribboned cord hang loose for me
the mane an old brown carpet strip
I watched him tack with care
and did not dare to say I hated how it felt
to me like cotton wool in Aspirin shiver
and baking in the sun I shiver as if
the future had come shadowed and adult
he smiles at my impatience holds out his hand
and I step up to his step

in the hut are his drawer of sharpened chisels
the carefully adjusted planes the line of lasts
from father down to me
leather wax and thread for him to repair shoes
I wear happily strike sparks from segs
click click my way into today.

# Learned Links

I am from edges
always at the brink of falling
out of the scheme and pattern fixed
on map and class and mind
I do not mind the looking
inwards to the assemblage
outwards to the travellers
they explore where I did not venture
for I am held by the gravity of
being alone being not of
not of the accepted orders

I may not or may
surrender to the desires or
surrender me to the centre
held pressed close warm protected
stare with them at the stranger
drive off any non-conformity
stamp down my waywardness
those who wander off are disinherited

for now they let me linger here
let me flirt from my molehill
I do not threaten nor question

I am tempted to the wilderness
value seeking treasures in my deserts
beyond learned paths
but there is comfort in holding on
the cards which litter my landscape

# Breathing

never forget to breathe
I do not mean the in-out necessity
of oxygen    the gasped sporting excess
the panted whisper of love

I mean the tasting of air
the view of sky and water savoured
delight of sea-birds and seals
breathe each breath flared into burning
to smoke and sizzle steaks
to the subtle aroma of lavender

do not ignore smell
nothing tastes touches sees hears
that does not live in scent carried
imprinted depths
inhale exhale
be

# Skimming stones at Coniston
*an evening reflection*

We stroll down from Ruskin's house,
in mid-summer, a sunlit walk.
I am frightened of saying the wrong thing,
do not point out foxgloves
which paint the garden,
their purple delight unspoken,

the harbour lies in shade, leaf clogged,
a shingle bank closes its mouth.
We discuss how neatly a boat would fit
in the stone walled channel.

At the beach beyond the buttress, the lake,
dark blue, tempting, promising cool relief.
My years of diving into deep waters are over
but not the need to break the surface calm.

I pick a stone for skimming,
index finger curled round its edge,
angle my body to the water,
send it flying, out, horizontal.
A single plop greets my efforts,
surface tension sliced, no hop and skip.
We laugh.  Nothing is said.
We return to the sun.

# At Home from Brantwood

darkness crowds in
suffocates sun on
Coniston Water as
the Steam Gondola
breathes in
to the pier

I
who live on here

smile my way aboard
bask in the warmth
of engine and sunshine
before the slow road home

on the hill is Brantwood
shadowed Ruskin long gone
but lingering

I hesitate
to leave
want some part of this
to infiltrate my
tomorrow
the etched hillside
the red sailed skiff
dreams of yesterday
to be real
when I wake

for now I shake
the kaleidoscope of memory
Finola and Felicia
take photographs

I touch the gilded dragon
on the prow
say it laughs

this is when time stops

I in familiar bed
sit writing